To Someone Special

Leah

From

Gramma

Love, From Grandma

Words of wisdom and hope
from grandmothers around the world.

෪ஐ

Compiled by Becky L. Amble

Published by Garborg's Heart 'n Home, Inc.
P.O. Box 20132
Bloomington, MN 55420

Cover photo used with permission of Dave and Louise Olsen
of Dave Olsen Photography, Inc.

ISBN 1-881830-23-3

Printed in the United States of America.

Dedication

To Grandma Betsey

Acknowledgments

All the grandmothers

Louise & Dave Olsen, Dave Olsen Photography, photo illustrators

Carol Ratelle Leach, editor

Jo Haugen, editor

Kimberly Kroubetz, editorial assistant

Unlimited Partners by Elizabeth & Robert Dole, published by Simon and Schuster

Norman Vincent Peale and Sybil Light of the Peale Center for Christian Living

A special thank you to Tessie for her diligent help, and to Dave and Louise for the photo illustration and hours of encouragement.

Thank you to all of the people who passed out my questionnaires, and especially to all of the women who took the time to write their advice. I wish we could have used everyone's material.

All of the grandmothers have given me permission to use their first name, initial of their last name, age, and either home town or current residence.

About the Author

Becky L. Amble

Becky L. Amble is an accomplished businesswoman, marketer, and researcher. She has been cited as a trendspotter by *The Wall Street Journal* and *USA Today*. She owns and operates Future Focus, a company that helps businesses develop growth strategies. She is also involved with several professional, civic, and community groups.

Becky grew up in North Dakota and now lives with her husband, Marshall Gravdahl, and two cats, Alexandra and Greta, in Woodbury, Minnesota.

Introduction

I believe God made grandmothers different from everyone else. They seem to love unconditionally—just as God does—holding us close to their hearts, wanting to protect and guide us. If we would only take the time to look and listen, they are always there for us.

The idea for this book developed out of my own business and workplace trend research as I noted several trends that indicated high levels of stress and uncertainty among Americans at every age. Since then, this project has really had a life of its own.

After sending out over 200 questionnaires to grandmothers throughout America, things started to happen. As questionnaires began returning, I would read the responses the day they arrived. I was not only struck by the love in their advice, but also by the appreciation each grandmother expressed to me for compiling this book and including them in it.

My own Grandma Betsey was a special person in my life—the only living grandparent I knew. When I was born, she was in her early 70s, and yet she never seemed as old as her years. Grandma was born in 1881 and grew up living on a farm in North Dakota—I know it was a different world then. Grandma lost two children who didn't live past the first few years of their lives, and she lived 30 years after Grandpa died. Even after weathering many tough times, Grandma was always calm, serene, and kind.

A courageous, strong woman, Grandma lived her last 30 years in darkness. You see, she was blind. Her life couldn't have been easy. We would go to visit her often, and she would come and stay with us. But most of the time Grandma lived alone in her house, cooking and cleaning—which I always thought was so amazing, since she was blind.

My best memories are of sitting with Grandma. She would rub my back, or we would sit, holding hands or play her "hand game"(where you alternate putting hands on top of each other's). She even taught me a little Norwegian. We never had to do anything special—just be together.

Grandma Betsey continues to be a guide for me—a gift from God. If your grandmother is still living, I hope you will take the time to be with her and enjoy her. If she has passed from this world, she can always be with you in spirit and memories.

Love, From Grandma is more than a book of advice, it is a book of love. Maybe your grandmother is in this book, or maybe she is speaking through one of these grandmothers.

Foreword

Our grandmothers often define the very best in us. Childhood memories of lessons learned at her knee become lessons to be followed in adulthood. The grandmother's position is an enviable one; all the good parts of listening and loving, playing and reading, praising and spoiling without the daily routine and problem solving. Her role allows nurturing and coaxing. From the vaulted position of grandmother, she can speak volumes about what's good and right and honest and pure. A grandmother can instill values and morals and truth through her wisdom and warmth.

Even today, when families are scattered, torn apart by the forces of our age, a grandmother can perform a service to youth. Even from a distance grandmothers communicate by mail, by fax, by phone—a sort of electronic knee. It misses some of the touch, the smell, and the feel, but the influence for good growth is still present.

My grandmother, Laura Peale, lived with her banker husband Samuel in the little rural Ohio town of Lynchburg, some 50 miles from Cincinnati. My brother Bob and I were dispatched by our parents to spend our summer vacation time in those healthful and supervised surroundings.

One memory stands out. We, of course, attended church every Sunday in the company of our grandmother. It was a small Methodist church in the style of the time. The sanctuary was square shaped with pews that formed a semicircle, one behind the other facing the pulpit and choir loft. Dressed in our scratchy Sunday best we would follow Grandmother into the church and to the familiar seats we always occupied. Grandma would separate the young brothers, one on either side of her, so as to forestall any troubling disturbance during the lengthy service. We squirmed and fretted. Before long Grandmother's soothing hand would rest on my knee as if to say, "it's only a little longer, Norman. Be still and listen to the great words of the Bible and hear those unforgettable hymns. This is important, Norman. You are learning about the goodness of God."

The soft and gentle hand of Grandmother was always gloved during church. And to this day I can smell the rich leather aroma of those black kid Sunday gloves, and I remember her—I remember all she taught me and I give thanks for the eternal truths I learned from my grandmother.

NORMAN VINCENT PEALE
Pawling, New York

Take care
of yourself.

Love, Grandma

Love, from Grandma

*Y*our future lies in your hands. Earn respect for who you are and what you stand for. Be strong about your beliefs and what you want to accomplish in life. Most of all, remember that you are a complete person and cannot look to others for happiness. To be happy and loved, love and be happy. Stay young in heart and share life with those who earn your love and respect. Don't look for happiness; happiness is inside you.

Jane W., 59, Minneapolis, Minnesota

*B*e responsible for all you say and do.

Mary D., 54, Peoria, Illinois

3

$\mathscr{A}$ positive attitude will help you through difficult times and make life better for you and others. Only you can control your attitude. Be honest with yourself as well as with others. Your friends will play an important part in your life, so select them carefully. The way you live your life can make a difference; caring and kindness are contagious. God made you unique and special and He loves you no matter what you do.

Eileen J., 62, Red Wing, Minnesota

$\mathscr{L}$earn how to give and take in order to live as peacefully as you can. Peace within is the best happiness we can achieve.

Leona H., 72, Billings, Montana

Take Care of Yourself

Love, from Grandma

*L*ife is short and involves hard work, so make it count for something. Remember that no matter what you do, it always affects someone else. Be ready not only to accept congratulations, but also responsibility. Use your mistakes as an opportunity to learn.

Jeanette S., 57, Monterey, California

*A*ccept yourself and value your uniqueness in the world. Be curious and continue to learn new things as long as you are able. Surround yourself with loving friends and family, and be in touch with your spirit. Love yourself so that you can love others.

Nell S., 58, Newman Grove, Nebraska

Always remember that you are unique; there is no one else like you. You are a child of a loving God and have inherent and infinite worth. Understanding that enables you to fulfill your unique potential, a condition for abundant living.

Christina S., 76, Spokane, Washington

Take Care of Yourself

Love, from Grandma

$\mathcal{A}$lways be honest with yourself first; it will extend automatically to others. Honesty keeps you in control and able to deal with all of life's situations.

Muriel O., 68, Thompson, North Dakota

$\mathcal{B}$e true to yourself always. Think highly of yourself and don't let the negative from others wear you down. Love other people as brothers and sisters. Be kind, courteous, and supportive. Meditate frequently on the Word of God and look to Him for strength and guidance.

Roxann M., 55, Mounds View, Minnesota

*N*owadays many are trying to influence you, usually for their own gain. It is vitally important that you think for yourself and hold fast to your beliefs.

Elizabeth L., 79, St. Paul, Minnesota

*L*ook at yourself in the mirror. Is this person your friend?
  You may fool the world down the pathway of years
  and get pats on your back as you pass,
    but your final reward will be heartache and tears
    if you have cheated the person in the glass.
Think for and be yourself.

Elaine R., 69, Naples, Maine

Take Care of Yourself

Love, from Grandma

*L*ife is a superb gift from God; treasure it! Make the most of every day and every opportunity. Each day is precious and filled with promise. Be optimistic; look for the "gold lining" in every cloud that temporarily hovers over you. Be loving and giving; all that you send into the lives of others comes back into your own.

Harriet B., 73, Lake Park, Minnesota

*F*ind your greatest contentment in your own company. Don't postpone the great adventure of reading biographies, history, short stories, and essays.

Mary G., 65, Omaha, Nebraska

$\mathcal{L}$ife is not always a bed of roses. Learn to accept the disappointments or things you cannot change, but stand tall and be proud of who you are.

Wilma H., 70, Tulare, South Dakota

$\mathcal{B}$e upfront with your feelings; don't sacrifice your feelings if you are being hurt for someone else's pleasure. Learn to laugh at your minor mistakes and to learn from the earth-shaking ones. Have a sense of humor and always be a good friend to the people who are good friends to you.

Sharon K., 50, Chicago, Illinois

Take Care of Yourself

Love, from Grandma

*E*mbrace life, love life; learn to cope with pain and adversity with courage. Be resilient. Be kind and compassionate. Be yourself.

Beverly B., 74, Edina, Minnesota

*K*eep a keen sense of humor; it will help you in many different situations and make you a more delightful person. When you are tempted to follow the crowd, believe in yourself. Be firm and don't be afraid to be different. Everyone admires an individual who has principles and stands up to be counted. Do what you espouse, because your credibility is in question. Be careful about what you want . . . you may get it!

Dodie P., 62, Ottawa, Canada

*$\mathcal{L}$ife is always good and sometimes it's better!
Be an optimist. Life is better when the glass is half full!*

Dodie P., 62, Ottawa, Canada

Take Care of Yourself

Love, from Grandma

Always be honest with yourself about how you feel, what you do, and your motives. Respect yourself so you can respect others. Be thoughtful about commitments so you can keep them—to yourself as well as others. Have good friends, animal and human, and make time for them, enjoy them. Listen to others, but weigh their input with your inner voice. Take small steps (and keep taking them) and big ones too. Have fun and enjoy your life; it's the only one you can live.

Pat L., 68, Princeton, Kentucky

Have confidence in yourself and don't be afraid to fail; sometimes you learn from your failures.

LaVonne H., 62, Moorhead, Minnesota

*L*earn to like yourself, and learn from your mistakes. Be a role model and take very good care of your reputation. Have self-respect and be self-disciplined. Never compromise your integrity. Know the value of *family*!

Penny B., 55, Irving, Texas

*O*nly you can determine what kind of life you will lead, so make it meaningful. I am so very proud of you. You have this one life; fill it with all the joy and happiness you can.

Helen B., 84, Roseville, Minnesota

Take Care of Yourself

Love, from Grandma

*D*o not pass up interesting opportunities. Learn from experience. Do not be afraid to take chances. Never look back and say, "If only I had done this." Life is a challenge; roll with the punches, take a deep breath, and try again.

Maryona J., 72, Miles City, Michigan

*J*ust be yourself; it's the way God made you and it's very fulfilling. Learn to control your own body and mind and you will become a strong, genuinely independent person. Don't act on impulse, but think things through. Make good choices.

Irene S., 57, Rothsay, Minnesota

*R*eflect on your life. Reflect also on God. Knowledge of God is not passive. Read, listen, and reflect. Align yourself with others who do this. It is better to love and suffer the pain of loss than to insulate yourself from others.

Betty M., 65, Rochester, Minnesota

*R*emain true to yourself. Remember, every tough situation you weather makes you stronger. Maintain a good sense of humor and laugh a lot, especially at yourself. Laughter makes living much more enjoyable.

Sharon D., 53, Washburn, Wisconsin

Take Care of Yourself

Love, from Grandma

*R*emember that character, dignity, and dependability are vital in life. Face your problems squarely; don't leave them for another day or for someone else to solve for you. Live each day as though it were your last, because some opportunities will not come your way again.

Norma T., 85, Reno, Nevada

*L*ive your life as if everything you do will be on the front page of the newspaper. Have faith and love your fellow man. Be determined and set examples for your own children. Show kindness to all.

Leta C., 70, Midland, Michigan

$\mathcal{T}$ake personal responsibility for your actions, your needs, and the solutions to your problems. Things will get better. What happens to you is less important than your reaction to events. Make no major decisions at night. Joy, optimism, and courage come with the morning. Happiness is your choice.
Feel gratitude—really feel it!

Becky Ann S., 74, West Lafayette, Indiana

$\mathcal{L}$ife is like a play; you have the leading role.
Make it an Oscar performance.

Kathie J., 50, Little Canada, Minnesota

Take Care of Yourself

Love, from Grandma

Smile. It's infectious.

Patricia N., 53, Fridley, Minnesota

*T*o "love your neighbor as yourself" starts by loving yourself and multiplies by sharing that love with others. Unconditional love brings a joyous energy that will surely bless your life with peace.

Lois V., 54, Clear Lake, Wisconsin

*B*e honest and fair with yourself as well as with others. Set short-term goals first with long-term expectations. Don't be disappointed if you have to make adjustments. Life is full of adjustments and you have to learn to be flexible. Have a good attitude and be happy.

Bonnie P., 54, Seattle, Washington

Take Care of Yourself

Love, from Grandma

*Y*our parents did the best for you that they could at the time, so don't blame them for your mistakes or possible unhappiness. You are liable for your own actions, right or wrong, and for your own happiness. Develop interests such as hobbies, volunteering, and sports, and you will never be bored or lonely.

Martha B., 72, Charlotte, Michigan

*E*verything you do, think, or say is very important. It does not matter what other people think about you. You know who you are and you know that you are very special. God loves you and I love you.

Pat D., 57, Mission, Texas

*Y*ou will get out of life what you put into it. I have several "rules for life":

Accentuate the positive. Look for the good in all situations, there is always some there. Concentrate on the good and play down the bad.

Do what comes naturally. Remember your roots. It's good to improve yourself, but never think that you are better than anyone else. Perhaps you were just lucky to have had better opportunities.

Keep it simple. Life is not meant to be complicated; people make it so. The simple things in life are best!

Karlene S., 59, Holyoke, Massachusetts

Take Care of Yourself

Love, from Grandma

*T*ake care of your whole self and encourage others to do the same.

Jane H., 68, St. Paul, Minnesota

*I*t takes a lifetime to build a good name, but one mistake to ruin it.

Dorothy S., 72, Menomonie, Wisconsin

*E*xperience your uniqueness. There is no one else on earth who has your combination of qualities. No one else on earth can make your observations or give your insights.

Vivian L., 73, Mora, Minnesota

Don't postpone joy in the beauty of life's rhythms.
Let no television program lure you from enjoying a sunset.

Mary G., 65, Omaha, Nebraska

Take Care of Yourself

*Take care
of your family
and friends.*

Love, Grandma

*K*eep family ties strong. You need your independence, but a close family circle can help you through the tough times and give you great joy.

Judy F., 59, Wolcott, Indiana

"*R*iches" does not mean money alone. Family, friendships, and health are riches to be desired more than money. Try to make the best of what you have and what life deals to you. Remember that your family is always here for support and advice, if requested. You are not alone.

Shirley R., 70, Dayton, Ohio

*K*now that your family loves you and that you can always go home, even if it's only in your memories.

Judy R., 48, Breckenridge, Minnesota

*A*lways try to communicate with your parents; they are smarter than you think. Loyalty to family and your country is very important.

Marge D., 58, Reynolds, Indiana

*B*e grateful to your parents; raising a child is not an easy task.

Alexia L., 64, Cleveland, Ohio

Take Care of Your Family and Friends

Love, from Grandma

Treasure your family;
they'll be there for you all your life.

Prudence B., 56, Rhinelander, Wisconsin

$\mathcal{C}$hoose a lifetime partner whose family background, values, and goals are similar to yours. The same sort of church background is very helpful. If you differ, discuss your differences and their importance to you before marriage. Be prepared for disagreements and try to resolve them; don't run away at the first obstacle. Living together before marriage is not a commitment, but a "cop-out" which does not necessarily lead to a long, happy marriage.

Martha B., 72, Charlotte, Michigan

$\mathcal{F}$amily and friends should be very important to you in your everyday life.

Jean K., 70, Fort Dodge, Iowa

Take Care of Your Family and Friends

Love, from Grandma

*F*amily is important. Enjoy the holidays and other special moments together.

Sherrill P., 52, West St. Paul, Minnesota

*H*elp others. Keep up your spiritual life. Marry the right person and enjoy life.

Jewell K., 82, Lynnfield, Massachusetts

*Y*our family loves you, so keep close to them through letters, telephone calls, and visits.

Lillian J., 78, Grand Forks, North Dakota

*T*hink before you act. Do not rush into relationships.

Helen H., 76, Chattanooga, Tennessee

*B*efore you commit to a life's partner, deal with the hard issues of spirituality and life goals with your eyes and mind open.

Jo G., 57, Red Lodge, Montana

*D*on't prepare so much for your wedding that you lose sight of the marriage.

Barbara M., 65, Mound, Minnesota

Take Care of Your Family and Friends

Love, from Grandma

Say "I love you" to those you do love.

Beatrice W., 62, Coon Rapids, Minnesota

When dating, always question whether you could be proud, happy, loving, and secure sharing life with that potential spouse. Looks and popularity are not the most important. Love, sincerity, and commitment are! Be selective, but realistic.

Jan A., 59, Prescott, Arizona

Value your family and friends,
and call your grandmother once a week!

Charlotte D., 60, Dayton, Ohio

Take Care of Your Family and Friends

Love, from Grandma

I want my example of living life—my walk before my five grandchildren—to be more than talk. Actions really do speak louder than words. I believe that children are a reflection of their parents, and grandchildren are the blessings, the reward of a job well done. We all need someone to follow, someone to look up to; that's the privilege of being a grandmother.

Gloria W., 69, Franklin Lakes, New Jersey

*T*reat your parents with respect and don't forget to be proud of where you came from.

LaVonne H., 62, Moorhead, Minnesota

First and foremost, let your children know you love them. Spoil and enjoy them from infancy to adulthood. But be firm with discipline and explain why if necessary. Try to do projects together (recreation, homework, cooking) even when your children are very young. Mine have always helped me make bread, cookies, and so on. Always praise their efforts, no matter how minor. And keep their imaginations alive. Children love to hear stories of the old days.

Elizabeth T., 70, St. Clair Shores, Michigan

Take Care of Your Family and Friends

*Take care
of others.*

Love, Grandma

Love, from Grandma

*A*ccept, encourage, and support how different we all are.

Judy A., 57, Baldwin, New York

*A*lways be honest and open. Have good communication with others. Treat all people with respect regardless of race or income. Remember that you are as good as any person, yet don't feel that you are better than anyone. Have faith in yourself and faith in the Lord and you will always have hope; anything that you pursue will be possible. Love yourself; don't depend on others to make you happy.

Irene H., 70, Avon, Minnesota

*H*ave compassion instead of rebellion, understanding instead of judgment, and above all, have love and caring. Always remember to respect people for themselves and not for what they can do for you.

Elizabeth S., 71, Kamuela, Hawaii

*B*e giving and forgiving. Seek out the good in people and love unconditionally. Be in control of your life, but don't try to control others.

Penny B., 55, Irving, Texas

Take Care of Others

Love, from Grandma

*B*e honest. Set high moral standards for yourself. Be considerate of others. Give of yourself. Care for people. Have good manners always.

LaVonne H., 62, Moorhead, Minnesota

*B*e loyal to your friends and keep a sense of humor. It helps with life's downs. Don't let silly misunderstandings cause major problems with friends or fellow workers. Life is not always fair, so you must be strong; don't be afraid to seek help. Be kind and try to see both sides of a problem. Above all, my dear grandchild, know that you are loved, and keep in touch.

Dorothy G., 71, Northville, Michigan

*T*rust your instincts; trust your judgment about people. Never be cruel. Love all the creatures of the world. Love others.
Love yourself.

Lee C., 75, Munich, Germany

*B*e loving and caring with people, for we are God's children. Care for His creation and the gifts we have been given; they are ours to borrow and pass on to others in better condition than when we found them, if possible.

Carolyn C., 62, Crystal, Minnesota

Take Care of Others

Be quick to say "I'm sorry" when you are to blame, and mean it! Be slow to judge others, for as you judge, so you will be judged. Be honest in all your dealings.

Agnes B., 85, San Jose, California

Enjoy all the gifts of life: nature, the arts, literature, food. But most of all enjoy the people—family, friends, community, and the chance acquaintance. Listen, listen to what they say, respect their thoughts, think upon them.

Jo G., 57, Red Lodge, Montana

*B*e yourself; don't try to be someone you are not. Have love and understanding for all people regardless of race or religion. Aim high. You can be anything you want; just be honest, sincere, dependable, and be a good friend.

Gwen M., 70, Hampton, New Hampshire

*D*on't waste your time or energy on hatred, bigotry, anger, or worry. Believe in the energizing power of love, and don't take yourself too seriously.

Janet W., 87, Naples, Florida

Take Care of Others

Be kind to everyone, especially older people.

Dorothy H., 83, Bemidji, Minnesota

$\mathscr{D}$on't always think about yourself. What you give, in return will make you feel much happier.

Shirley P., 71, Roseville, Minnesota

$\mathscr{F}$ill yourself with love, grace, warmth, and sensitivity. Always be loyal. Once a friend, always a friend. Do something for someone else every day of your life, preferably anonymously. Remember, God wants us to love others.

Gracie G., 68, Alpena, Michigan

$\mathscr{L}$et yourself be God's instrument of His love for all people.

Marianne W., 64, St. Paul, Minnesota

Take Care of Others

Love, from Grandma

$\mathscr{K}$eep in contact with friends and family; know that they are there to support you in any way that you need. Make new friends, too, to enrich and broaden your life.

Carol P., 57, Harrisville, Rhode Island

$\mathscr{M}$anners are very important and will help you throughout your life. A smile and a friendly manner plus a genuine "thank you" can save the day!

Ida K., 70, St. Paul, Minnesota

$\mathcal{S}$how kindness to others who need your help and guidance. Be a caring person who is full of love.

Beverly T., 56, Acton, Massachusetts

$\mathcal{T}$reat other people as you would like them to treat you. Care for people's feelings; we are all in process.

Betty M., 65, Rochester, Minnesota

$\mathcal{L}$earn from the mistakes and experiences of others as well as from your own.

Mary D., 54, Peoria, Illinois

Take Care of Others

Love, from Grandma

$\mathcal{L}$earn to get along with your fellow human beings. *Loving, caring,* and *sharing* are good watchwords for life.

Beverly B., 74, Edina, Minnesota

$\mathcal{L}$ive your life with a positive attitude and surround yourself with positive people. Treat everyone you meet, young or old, with kindness and an open mind.

Edith G., 65, Methuen, Massachusetts

$\mathcal{L}$ive your life as a helpful person. Be loving, forgiving, and helpful at all times.

Lillian L., 78, Baltimore, Maryland

*G*et to know people of many races, religions, and cultures, and learn to appreciate their uniqueness. Share your ideas, dreams, time, talents, and material goods. Develop your ability to be a friend, to be caring and supportive. Above all, give God the glory in all good things that come your way.

Mae Lou T., 60, Beresford, South Dakota

*D*o not let unkind thoughts become unkind words.

Patricia B., 56, Palmer, Alaska

Take Care of Others

Love, from Grandma

*L*ove, caring, and personal relationships are more important than accumulating things. Possessions can't make you happy. You make your own happiness.

Mary C., 57, Hudson, Wisconsin

*N*ever go against your good judgment to follow a peer or group in the wrong direction. Be strong, do right, and enjoy a successful life. Be considerate of others, especially the less fortunate.

Thestina T., 84, Grand Forks, North Dakota

*O*nly God can judge you, not your neighbors.

Carmen K., 61, Shoreview, Minnesota

*H*ave a vital interest in what is happening around you, and try to make this world a better place by what you do.

Norma T., 85, Reno, Nevada

*R*egardless of how others treat you, think of how you would like to be treated and follow that path.

Ethel S., 75, Woodbury, Connecticut

*T*ry to walk in someone else's shoes to understand how he or she feels.

LaVonne H., 62, Moorhead, Minnesota

Take Care of Others

Love, from Grandma

$\mathcal{I}$f "everyone is doing it," don't. Think! Think! Think!

Becky Ann S., 74, West Lafayette, Indiana

$\mathcal{T}$ake support from your family and be there for them. Happiness comes from being concerned for the welfare of others. Don't be selfish!

Jean K., 70, Fort Dodge, Iowa

$\mathcal{R}$emember those who are hurting and reach out to them in appropriate ways.

Marlys S., 70, Sun City West, Arizona

The more you give of yourself, the more you will receive in return. Think before you speak. Be kind and, above all else, don't be judgmental. Unkind and hurtful words last a lifetime. Saving face is less important than saving a friendship. Enjoy yourself, but never at someone else's expense. All people are God's children. We are in a diverse and interesting world. Be open and inquiring to learn more—never stop learning. Bring your hurts and pain home to those who love you. Those who really love you will be there for you.

Dodie P., 62, Ottawa, Canada

Take Care of Others

Love, from Grandma

To have a friend, you must be one. Friends of all ages make life interesting. Laugh and have fun. Be responsible for your actions. Do something to help others. There are so many good causes and so few volunteers.

Lillian J., 78, Grand Forks, North Dakota

Be open and honest with people. Work hard and apply yourself, but don't forget to enjoy life and your relationships. Try to see something positive in each and every person you come in contact with. Make friends with people from all walks of life and you will be a terrific adult.

Dorothy B., 59, St. Paul, Minnesota

*S*how love, patience, and compassion. It is in giving, not getting, that our lives are blessed. Remember that a life worth living is filled with giving and forgiving.

Ruth R., 88, Fort Dodge, Iowa

*W*e only get one chance at this life, so give it your best shot. Live life to the fullest without hurting others as you go. Be kind, generous, and considerate to everyone you meet along the way.

Adele P., 61, St. Paul, Minnesota

Take Care of Others

*Take care
of your spirit.*

Love, Grandma

Love, from Grandma

*N*urture your spiritual health even more than your physical health. Seek God, love God, love yourself; then you can love others. Believe in the triumph of good always. Express gratitude to your family, friends, associates, and God.

Becky Ann S., 74, West Lafayette, Indiana

*S*tay close to God, because with Him all things are possible. Keep prayer in your life and read inspirational material.

Marion D-H., 51, Knoxville, Tennessee

*Y*ou are a child of a loving God and have inherent and infinite worth.

Christina S., 76, Spokane, Washington

*S*ay your prayers every day. Strong faith in God can pull you through the darkest of times.

Patricia B., 56, Palmer, Alaska

*P*lace spiritual values above everything.

Eleanor B., 73, Golden Valley, Minnesota

*W*e were all made by the same God and He loves us all equally. Can we do any less? Love your God, love your family, love your fellow-man, and it will follow that you will love yourself.

Karlene S., 59, Holyoke, Massachusetts

Take Care of Your Spirit

Love, from Grandma

*H*ave an abiding faith in our loving God who created all things. Choose Jesus, the way of love, and you choose abundant, eternal life.

Marj C., 74, Atwood, Kansas

*D*are to be guided by the Holy Spirit. God will be with you in your decision-making.

Gerda L., 79, Albion, Nebraska

*I*f you start your day with prayer, God will lead and guide you. Remember, God is on call twenty-four hours a day.

Arleen K., 71, Thompson, North Dakota

Think highly of yourself, and stay close to God. Then you will have good friends and be able to resist temptation.

Elizabeth W., 79, Sebastian, Florida

Always carry God's love with you. It will enable you to understand and to forgive. Appreciate all that He has given you.

Ruth C., 77, Sioux Falls, South Dakota

It gives you a good feeling to go to church.

Dorothy H., 83, Bemidji, Minnesota

Take Care of Your Spirit

Love, from Grandma

ife in all forms is a gift from God. If life seems too complicated, return to your childhood faith. You will see the right path to take.

Muriel O., 68, Thompson, North Dakota

*E*veryone you meet is made in God's image. Give them the respect and the dignity they deserve as His children. Nurture your own relationship with God. Spiritual nuturing is every bit as important as physical and mental nurturing.

Sandy L., 47, Plymouth, Minnesota

*A*s a child of God your priorities should be: Daily Devotions, Prayer and Praise, Ten Percent Tithe, and Weekly Worship.

Elaine K., 63, Cottage Grove, Minnesota

Take Care of Your Spirit

Love, from Grandma

*S*tay close to the Lord; He'll give you guidance and wisdom. You have to take time to receive it. If you do there will be no challenge in your life that His counsel cannot help you to solve.

Helen B., 72, Minneapolis, Minnesota

*D*evelop a strong spiritual life. It will ease the problems and difficulties of life and enhance its joys and successes.

Jo G., 57, Red Lodge, Montana

*L*ove God, then love and care for yourself, your family, and others—in this order. If you truly love God and yourself, everything else will fall into place.

Kathy P., 56, New Market, Alabama

*T*ake time to be quiet and talk to God. Enjoy the beauty of creation and preserve it. Above all, give God the glory in all good things that come your way.

Mae Lou T., 60, Beresford, South Dakota

*G*od made you unique and special, one of a kind, and He loves you no matter what.

Eileen J., 62, Red Wing, Minnesota

*W*alk with God. Life is difficult and He has much to teach as you walk through, and grow because of, those hard times.

Gerry L., 57, Grand Forks, North Dakota

Take Care of Your Spirit

Love, from Grandma

$\mathcal{T}$he best advice I can give is to have faith, hope, and charity. Have *faith* in God, a personal relationship with our living Savior, and faith in yourself. Have *hope* for the future and take a positive approach to everything. And have *charity* to share yourself and your talents with others and to give help to those who are in need.

Olive B., 62, Hatton, North Dakota

$\mathcal{A}$ttend Sunday School and church. Believe in God. He will keep you on the right path and help you through all your trials.

Beatrice W., 62, Coon Rapids, Minnesota

God's love is ours always.

Jackie O., 51, Dawson, Minnesota

Take Care of Your Spirit

Love, from Grandma

*L*ife is a superb gift from God; treasure it! Make the most of every day and every opportunity.

Harriet B., 73, Lake Park, Minnesota

*T*he only answer for living is found in the Bible, in Proverbs 3:5–6. My paraphrase: We need to trust in the Lord with all our hearts and not rely on our own human fallible understanding. We should in all our ways acknowledge Him as our Supreme God, and then we will know that He will direct our paths.

Louise W., 63, Hollidaysburg, Pennsylvania

*L*ive life each day fully for God. Greet each morning with the prayer, "Lord, what are You and I going to do together today? I'm reporting for duty." You'll never be bored.

Pearl S., 62, Houston, Texas

*I*f you make mistakes, ask God to forgive you and accept that you are forgiven. Put a high value on yourself. You are what God made you to be.

Irene S., 57, Rothsay, Minnesota

*P*rayer changes things. Trust in the Lord.

Ruth R., 88, Fort Dodge, Iowa

Take Care of Your Spirit

Love, from Grandma

$\mathscr{B}$ecome acquainted with God. Talk to Him as you walk, dream, or pray. He listens.

Allegra V., 71, Midland, Michigan

$\mathscr{A}$lways take joy in the little things God gives you, along with His greater gifts. Don't keep your relationship with God too sacred. Talk to Him when you're in the shower or stuck in traffic.

Judy R., 48, Breckenridge, Minnesota

$\mathscr{G}$od loves you and I love you.

Pat D., 67, Mission, Texas

*T*reasure honesty, both in listening to the Spirit within and in dealing with all people. Build a strong and personal relationship with God. Do all you can to deepen that bond of love and trust between the Creator and yourself.

Marianne W., 64, St. Paul, Minnesota

*G*o to church and find friends there. Try to find a good community to live in. Start out, if possible, in a place where you have friends and relatives.

Marion M., 75, Canby, Oregon

Take Care of Your Spirit

Love, from Grandma

*W*hen you were born you became a gift to your family.
You are a special child of God.

Ella B., 62, Trondheim, Norway

*A*lways think of yourself as loved by God, who *is* Love.

Margaret Mary M., 70, Morris, Minnesota

*W*e are God's workmanship!

Mary D., 51, Carrollton, Texas

Count each day as a new beginning, the first day of the rest of your life, while remembering to show reverence for God.

Norma H., 70, Lenox, Massachusetts

Take Care of Your Spirit

*Take care
of your future.*

Love, Grandma

Love, from Grandma

*N*ever say "never." We have no idea what the future holds for us.

Ethel S., 75, Woodbury, Connecticut

*B*e cheerful and friendly to people. Have good work ethics; show up for work and be on time. Don't stand around and gossip, but try to keep busy. Have good people skills and communication skills. Obtain an education that will help you to support yourself. Computer skills are important in this day and age. Do not chew gum at work.

Agnes S., 84, Cavalier, North Dakota

*K*now your craft and do it better than the others.

Geraldine H., 79, Kansas City, Missouri

$\mathcal{B}$e honest and considerate; it will gain you the trust of others. Without it you have nothing. Money won't buy you happiness— only a few material comforts. Friends, family, and time for yourself should come before work.

Sandra G., 52, Princeton, Minnesota

$\mathcal{T}$he world you live in is full of opportunities to fulfill your every dream. You will be tempted in many ways, but follow your good common sense and don't be intimidated by anyone.

Dorothy S., 72, Menomonie, Wisconsin

Take Care of Your Future

Love, from Grandma

*D*o what you want to do. Further your education no matter what occupation you choose. You may change your mind after studying awhile.

Helen O., 79, Preston, Minnesota

*D*on't expect the "good life" to be handed to you on a silver platter. Prepare yourself for life by getting a good education. Have goals and do your utmost to achieve them. Don't squander anything—your health, your resources, or the good old common sense you inherited. Don't take any of the above for granted. You can't buy them at any price. They are God's gift to you.

Gladys S., 88, Grand Forks, North Dakota

*S*ince a great deal of your time will be spent at your job, make the most of it. Do your fair share, be on time, don't whine or complain, be neat and clean. Be kind to those less fortunate than yourself. Your rewards will be many.

Kay F., 53, Staples, Minnesota

*D*evelop a positive attitude and expect to achieve success. Your attitudes are self-fulfilling. Having a positive attitude will help you be successful.

Ginger J., 58, Portland, North Dakota

Take Care of Your Future

Love, from Grandma

*L*ife is not necessarily meant to be easy, and there is no guarantee that you will be taken care of. Work hard and plan for your future, even into retirement. But set aside some time for fun and relaxation; it makes the rest easier.

Judy F., 59, Wolcott, Indiana

*L*ife is the happiest and the most worthwhile if you savor planting the seeds, watching them grow, and nurturing them, not just picking the fruit and the flowers.

Barbara M., 65, Mound, Minnesota

*L*ife will have its trials, its ups and downs. With optimism and consideration of others, life can be very good.

Hildegard S., 65, Munich, Germany

*D*ecide what you really want to do with your life, then set goals so you can achieve it.

Betty S., 70, Ponca City, Oklahoma

*B*e clear about who you are and why you are here. Have fun every day. Learn from everything you do. Ask plenty of questions.

Betsy B., 48, Duluth, Minnesota

Take Care of Your Future

Love, from Grandma

Hold on to your dreams. If you believe you can do it, you will. Set goals and take a step toward them each day.

Marion D-H., 51, Knoxville, Tennessee

*M*y advice is to make the best of what you have. Learn to handle your own money and spend it wisely. Whatever you choose to do, do it well. Be fair in all your dealings and business matters. Be a true friend, a good neighbor, and a hard worker.

Irene H., 85, Casselton, North Dakota

*W*ork hard at whatever job or endeavor you choose. Do not undertake more than you can handle, whether commitments or credit.

Jane H., 66, St. Paul, Minnesota

Take Care of Your Future

Love, from Grandma

$\mathscr{B}$e true to yourself and the principles you have been taught. Try to approach life as a great gift and to have enormous fun and enjoyment. You are a reflection of the people who have loved and raised you.

Karleen P., 57, Hudson, Wisconsin

$\mathscr{N}$ever waver in your pursuits. Reach for the stars; many things are possible. The road of life brings many unexpected twists and turns. It is at these times that you must not swerve. Perhaps around the bend the road of life will again become straight.

Frances R., 89, Holyoke, Massachusetts

*W*hen you fall for any reason, pick yourself up and start anew; after setbacks, you can go forward to a better existence. Keep on learning, which is the key to success.

Patricia N., 53, Fridley, Minnesota

*Y*ou can't have everything overnight. Work diligently and you will begin to see the rewards. Remember your roots. Worship regularly as you were brought up to do.

S. Jeanette F., 69, Grand Forks, North Dakota

Take Care of Your Future

Love, from Grandma

*W*hen we were children, we were so eager for life to move along quickly. Go slowly. Everything happens in its time. Life should not be fleeting. It should be slow, rich, and ideally, long.

Kathie J., 50, Little Canada, Minnesota

*Y*ou are a very special person. Strive to be the best at whatever profession you may choose. Use your God-given talents, and remember that, no matter your age, your grandparents will be there for you.

Lois W., 59, Columbus, Wisconsin

*A*lways save a percent of your income regardless of how small the amount may be. Tomorrow always comes; the sun keeps rising and setting.

Flo E., 56, Bismarck, North Dakota

I wish I had learned early in life to set goals. You need short-term and long-term goals in your career, in your personal life, and in your spiritual life. Remember, your goals are yours alone, and only you can achieve them! If you miss your target, don't be discouraged. Bounce back! Re-evaluate, reorganize, and proceed!

Jan A., 59, Prescott, Arizona

Take Care of Your Future

Love, from Grandma

*L*ife is a wonderful thing. You have been given abilities; now you must choose how you are going to live your life.

Ruth M., 84, Auburn, Washington

*Y*ou have finally reached that point in your young life when you answer only to yourself. Sounds wonderful, doesn't it? Or does it feel a little scary? Remember, you have two of the most wonderful resources to turn to for encouragement, help, understanding, and most of all, love: your parents and God. When life gets tough, they will be there for you.

Mary Ann Z., 61, Woodbury, Minnesota

*L*ive life *now!* Do all you can today with no financial debts! Spend only what you can afford.

Ruth B., 87, Woodmere, New York

*B*e happy when someone else wins the race, the game, the money.

Cathy C., 54, Minnetonka, Minnesota

Take Care of Your Future

Take care
of your values
and beliefs.

Love, Grandma

Love, from Grandma

*A*s much as possible, live by the Golden Rule and the Ten Commandments.

Jewell K., 82, Lynnfield, Massachusetts

*Y*ou can't go wrong with old-fashioned morality based on the teachings of the Bible.

Mary Jane B., 75, Chicago, Illinois

*B*e fair. Have good morals. Don't follow the crowd if it goes against your moral code. Don't be afraid to say no!

Mary C., 62, Forest Lake, Minnesota

Examine and define your values. Do not choose to do anything that violates your values. Decisions will come more easily once this framework is in place.

Myrna N., 56, Plankinton, South Dakota

Take Care of Your Values

Love, from Grandma

*H*ave good moral values and standards. Life makes sense only if we can relate it to lasting values.

Irene H., 70, Avon, Minnesota

*H*old on to your convictions and don't be afraid to stand by them in a crowd. Don't allow peer pressure to dictate your moves. Love yourself and like your actions.

Pat J., 59, Lake View, Iowa

I believe in the old-fashioned values of honesty, morality, compassion, reliability, and responsibility.

Martha B., 72, Charlotte, Michigan

*K*eep your word at any cost.

Priscilla G., 48, Camarillo, California

*L*et your conscience be your guide. Don't allow a friend to talk you into doing something you know is wrong. You can say no! Be your own person.

Beatrice W., 62, Coon Rapids, Minnesota

*L*ife is very short. Decide how you want to live it. Set your own direction and go for it!

Mary C., 57, Hudson, Wisconsin

Take Care of Your Values

Love, from Grandma

It takes a much stronger person to say "no" than to follow the crowd. Set your goals high. "When the going gets tough, the tough get going" is a good motto.

Mildred S., 75, Grand Forks, North Dakota

Don't let others make decisions for you. Because today's society is so culturally, morally, and economically diverse, we must always evaluate our beliefs carefully before making decisions. We must learn to understand and respect others' values, yet feel proud of our own values.

E. Irene T., 69, New Hope, Minnesota

*M*y primary advice is "don't procrastinate."

Elizabeth L., 79, St. Paul, Minnesota

*L*ive each day as a gift; you can't get it back, but you'll have a chance tomorrow to do it over.

Marcella M., 78, Sioux City, Iowa

*P*lace spiritual values above everything.

Eleanor B., 73, Golden Valley, Minnesota

Take Care of Your Values

Love, from Grandma

$\mathscr{R}$emember the moral standards you were raised with.

Helen H., 76, Chattanooga, Tennessee

$\mathscr{S}$tand up for what you believe.

Carol P., 57, Harrisville, Rhode Island

$\mathscr{T}$hough it is nice to be well thought of and respected, don't compromise your own values and ideas just to gain someone else's acceptance.

Sharon K., 50, Chicago, Illinois

*V*alues are hard to keep in perspective, but to me they make our lives what they are. The words of advice that top my list are these:

Unselfishness. This is what "earns" love from family and gains you many friends. You can't live without them.

Honesty. When you are one of the oldies you'll not need to regret having hurt someone along the way.

Faith. This is the most important. There is Someone who cares very much about what happens to you.

Marge B., 74, Austin, Minnesota

Take Care of Your Values

Love, from Grandma

Enduring values are better than pleasure for the moment.

Carolyn C., 62, Crystal, Minnesota

$\mathscr{G}$reet each day as a wonderful new challenge and a precious gift. You won't have time for preoccupation with past negatives.

Pat S., 71, Largo, Florida

$\mathscr{F}$amily and friends are all-important. As you make choices today, consider how they will affect you tomorrow. Be true to your values.

Jean V., 71, Baldwin, Wisconsin

Take Care of Your Values

*Take care
of all the rest.*

Love, Grandma

Love, from Grandma

*T*ake time each day to appreciate life and to have some fun and laughter! Find the humor and joy in every day!

Carol P., 57, Harrisville, Rhode Island

*A*lways wear clean underwear in case you're in an accident.

Florence B., 82, Rhinelander, Wisconsin

*B*e cautious, but not so much that you don't take chances or have fun while living a full life. Be sure to give by volunteering. Do as much traveling as possible.

Virginia M., 62, Dunwoody, Georgia

$\mathcal{D}$o lots of reading. Cultivate a hobby or something to do when you're alone, such as reading. Nourish your spiritual life through books and prayer. Do something fun for exercise and eat healthy foods.

Jeanne C., 74, St. Paul, Minnesota

$\mathcal{D}$on't live for tomorrow. Enjoy each day to the fullest. Don't waste time on regrets or guilt; we all have them. Never hide secrets by telling lies; they multiply. Focus on the wonderful things that you can experience every day. Take time to notice all of the beauty around you, and remember that this is a gift.

Allegra V., 71, Midland, Michigan

Take Care of All the Rest

Love, from Grandma

*D*ress and act respectfully. Keep your house and surroundings clean and neat. Open a savings account and save regularly in order to have funds for an emergency. Remember to go to church regularly.

Julia B., 72, Pensacola, Florida

*T*hings and events will sometimes not go your way. Be a good contestant (a good loser, if necessary) and, above all, keep your sense of humor.

D. Jane H., 69, Midland, Michigan

*H*ave fun. Don't take yourself or anyone else too seriously.

Sue S., 58, Roseville, Minnesota

*E*njoy life and get involved in several extracurricular activities. Be conscious of and responsible for your actions. Stand up for your rights, but also know when to cooperate. Respect and consider the advice of others, especially your parents.

Ann K., 54, Wales, North Dakota

*L*earn to rejoice in the daily ordinary things and occurrences. Stay hope-filled.

Marie G., 72, Lamberton, Minnesota

*S*trengthen your mind continuously.

Roxann M., 55, Mounds View, Minnesota

Take Care of All the Rest

Love, from Grandma

Enjoy nature and appreciate the beauty it provides. You will only have one lifetime. Fill it full of good memories!

Betty B., 79, Sun City, Arizona

Eat well and exercise. It is good to know how to delay pleasure. Pleasure is necessary, but it's not everything.

Betty M., 65, Rochester, Minnesota

First rule for life: "Don't sweat the small stuff." Second rule for life: "Everything is small stuff."

Charlotte D., 60, Dayton, Ohio

Give to the world the best you have and the best will come back to you. Practice honesty, unselfishness, fairness, compassion, integrity, self-discipline, and belief in God.

Margaret F., 81, Melbourne, Florida

Take Care of All the Rest

Love, from Grandma

*E*xperience as many new adventures as you can.

Karol W., 53, Everett, Washington

*H*ealth and happiness are not guaranteed in this life. Recognize the good things and take time to appreciate them. It's not what you have or how much you have but who you have to share it with. You have to think for yourself. You must make your own decisions, knowing that you will have to live with them. Also, how you feel today is not how you will always feel about things. Your understanding of life will change throughout your life.

Lorelie A., 55, Hastings, Minnesota

*L*ife is a mystery to be lived, not a puzzle to be solved.

Kaye O., 67, Chicago, Illinois

I believe that life is an exciting adventure. There are valleys and peaks and we must have a zest for life, a positive attitude, and faith in God. With these things we can know, even in our most trying times, that there is a light at the end of the tunnel. Look for the good in others and, most importantly, have confidence in yourself.

Karen W., 48, Detroit, Michigan

Take Care of All the Rest

Love, from Grandma

I have always tried to set a good example and to give advice through action and not through words. I think it lasts longer and is more effective.

Tillie T., 81, Newman Grove, Nebraska

Keep fit. Keep your body healthy. Health and strength are a precious gift, so avoid drugs, alcohol, and sex. Throughout life spread a bit of sunshine, some joy, and a little laughter, and—oh yes, share your tears. Love is the only thing that abides forever.

Ruth R., 88, Fort Dodge, Iowa

*F*ind balance in your life. Don't put all your eggs in one basket. Work, leisure, worship, and learning are all part of life; to concentrate on one aspect and ignore the rest is a big mistake.

Sandy L., 47, Plymouth, Minnesota

*L*ife is an adventure and a journey. Good things and some not-so-good things will happen to you on your lifetime journey. Remember, it's not what happens to you that counts. It's how you choose to react and think.

Rubye E., 62, Edina, Minnesota

Take Care of All the Rest

Love, from Grandma

$\mathcal{L}$ife is very fragile. Live each day as if it were your last on this earth.

Marlys S., 70, Sun City West, Arizona

$\mathcal{S}$tay busy. Keep inquiring about life and its good options. Dress neatly.

Eline B., 67, St. Paul, Minnesota

$\mathcal{L}$ife is beautiful at any age; tough, but beautiful. Keep a positive attitude. It will get you over the rough times, and you will live longer.

Gloria W., 69, Franklin Lakes, New Jersey

$\mathcal{L}$ife is difficult, but also wonderful. With love, patience, self-confidence, and faith you can overcome its traumas. Life will return to you what you have given of yourself.

Lorraine W., 80, Minneapolis, Minnesota

$\mathcal{I}$f you find yourself in an unpleasant or harmful situation, leave or get out *immediately*!

Patricia B., 56, Palmer, Alaska

$\mathcal{N}$ow that you are an adult, make sure you try to make this world a better place by your actions. Lead an honest life and you'll never have to backtrack or cover up your wrongs.

Carol B., 53, Elk River, Minnesota

Take Care of All the Rest

Love, from Grandma

*L*ive life, smell the roses, travel, laugh, and
appreciate all that God has given you.

Ruth C., 77, Sioux Falls, South Dakota

*M*aintain a balance of spiritual, mental, and physical activities in life; each is important. Have fun and laugh!

Marion D-H., 51, Knoxville, Tennessee

*Y*ou never have to remember what you've said if you tell the truth. No matter what you have, little or much, share with others. Support charities to the best of your ability.

Shirley R., 70, Dayton, OH

*Y*ou get out of life what you put into life. Your attitude toward life is in your control. Be positive, but also realistic.

Mary H., 62, New Ulm, Minnesota

Take Care of All the Rest

Love, from Grandma

*M*ake use of the abilities God has given you. Every problem has a solution. Enjoy what is beautiful and believe that as you give to the world, so the world will give to you. Here is a saying that I like:

> Do more than exist, live.
> Do more than read, absorb.
> Do more than touch, feel.
> Do more than hear, listen.
> Do more than look, observe.
> Do more than listen, understand.

Janahn E., 79, Newman Grove, Nebraska

*P*rotect your virginity for marriage. Seek good things in order to enjoy a fruitful life.

Mary Jane B., 75, Chicago, Illinois

*A*lways finish what you start. Spend no more than you have. Save 10%. Give 10%. (Use the 10/10/80 plan.) Remember, you are never alone.

Betty H., 68, Nekoosa, Wisconsin

*S*hare what you have and you will always be happy. Happiness is not having what you want, but wanting what you have.

Marian M., 70, Roseville, Minnesota

Take Care of All the Rest

Love, from Grandma

*N*ow that you are on your own, don't forget the rules from home. Your parents cannot see the things you are doing, but God can. Your parents trust you. Live up to their trust. Life can be exciting and fun; be sure you live it the right way. There is never a problem too small or too big to call home about. You can count on us!

Arleen K., 71, Thompson, North Dakota

*O*ur lives are in process every moment, which means change is ever present. Don't be afraid of change. We usually don't recognize the really important moments in our lives until it's too late. Enjoy each day. People often pass up the moment, looking too far ahead. We only really have right now.

Gerry C., 67, Phoenix, Arizona

Take care of the little things. The big things take care
of themselves!

Jackie O., 51, Dawson, Minnesota

Patience is the ability to count down before blasting off.
Patience is more than just holding back the negative emotions of
anger, irritation, or hostility; it is being calm. Upsetting, irritating
circumstances are bound to be a part of your day-to-day life.
Forewarned is forearmed, so try to retreat to your calm.

Nellie M., 93, Kanawha, Iowa

Take Care of All the Rest

Love, from Grandma

Try to have a garden wherever you live. Even if it's a pot on the front step. Plants are good for you and it's good to get your hands dirty now and then. Make sure you have music, too. I don't care what kind it is as long as you like it. Eat right and exercise. Have fun. The kind of fun that makes you feel good. Clean fun, like a really good game of golf. Get a dog. You'll always have someone to come home to that really wants to see you. Find a friend, a real friend you can confide in. You won't need a psychiatrist. (The dog will help too.) When you find that friend, let him or her confide in you. When you look for the love of your life, don't look so much at the outside. Look with your heart, and when you marry, do so with the idea that you're doing this for life. When you lose people you love, grieve. Then live, and always take joy in the little things God gives you, along with His greater gifts. Care about others. Not just with your money, but with your time. Laugh a lot.

Judy R., 48, Breckenridge, Minnesota

*T*aking care of yourself is a wonderful way to learn and grow. Have fun, enjoy your accomplishments, and appreciate the smallest, as well as the greatest, accomplishments. Learn from your mistakes—you will make many, of course. Remember, when you have tough times and are feeling down and discouraged, that you are loved and that you can reach out for help. Help in many forms is always available to you.

Carol P., 56, Harrisville, Rhode Island

Take Care of All the Rest

Love, from Grandma

WHAT IS A GRANDMA?

The following was written by a third
grader for a school assignment:

A grandma is a lady who has no children of her own, so she likes other people's little girls. A grandfather is a man grandmother. He goes for walks with the boys and they talk about fishing and things like that. Grandmas don't have anything to do except be here. They are so old they should not play hard. It is enough if they drive us to the supermarket where the pretend horse is and have lots of dimes ready, or if they take us for walks they should slow down past pretty things like leaves and caterpillars. They should never say "hurry up." Usually they are fat, but not too fat. They wear glasses and funny underwear. They can take their teeth and gums off. It is better if they don't typewrite or play cards, except with us. They don't have to be smart, only answer questions like why dogs hate cats and how come God isn't married. They don't talk baby-talk like visitors do because it is hard to understand. When they read to us they don't skip words or mind if it is the same story again. Everybody should try to have a grandma, especially if they don't have a television, because grandmas are the only grownups who have got time.

Thank you to Grandmother Patricia B. of Palmer, Alaska for sending this to us.

Take Care of All the Rest

Love, from Grandma

*G*randmothers come in all different shapes, colors, sizes, and personalities, yet each one has her own valuable wisdom to share with her loved ones. Use the following pages to record your grandmother's unique insights or take time to reflect on memories of her.

Love, from Grandma

Love, from Grandma

_____
_____
_____
_____
_____
_____
_____
_____
_____
_____
_____
_____
_____
_____
_____
_____

Love, from Grandma

Love, from Grandma

Love, from Grandma

Love, from Grandma

Love, from Grandma

Love, from Grandma